Special Stories Publishing

www.specialstories.net

Acknowledgements

Many thanks to Kieran, my father Michael, my brother George and my extended family and friends. Special thanks too to my uncle Liam Gaynor, Liz O'Donoghue, Eva Byrne and the Louth County Enterprise Board for their endless encouragement, support and invaluable advice.

Special thanks also to Dr. Gerard Molloy Ph.D C.Psychol. whose time and effort with this project was so greatly appreciated.

About the Illustrator

Aileen Murphy is an artist who lives in Dublin. She grew up in the country side of Co. Wicklow and then studied in the The National College of Art and Design. Now she works in her studio in Dublin City drawing and making various 3D art. Aileen's artwork usually relates to Fairy tales, girlhood motifs and wacky dreams. In the future she wants to travel to Iceland, illustrate many more children's books, have many art exhibitions and eventually move closer to the country side so she can own a dog and a vegetable garden.

To read more about the special stories collection, visit the Special Stories website at:
www.specialstories.net

for my brother George , Liz O'D and Liz D

Hi! my name is **Lucy**. I am five years old.

My favourite creatures are goldfish. I love their bright orange colour and how they swim around their tanks and never go to sleep!

Even though I'm the same as every other boy and girl I have something called Diabetes. Diabetes is a hard word to say but when I break it down it sounds like this – "Di – ah – beet – ees", which isn't so hard at all.

All boys and girls need to be careful not to eat too many sugary things so that they keep their teeth white and their bodies healthy.

But when a person has diabetes they have to be even more careful.

When a boy or girl has diabetes they have to take a special type of medicine called insulin. If they take their insulin every day they can have fun and play with their friends as much as they like.

Doctors or grown ups use a needle to put the insulin into our bodies. When we get older we can learn how to do this for ourselves.

The very first time that I saw a needle I wasn't very brave! I was afraid that the needle would hurt and make me cry.

The doctor promised that it would be over in no time at all and I should try hard to be a brave girl.

The needle felt a bit strange going into my arm at first but it was over in a second, and it wasn't sore at all!

One sunny day when I was in my classroom with my friends, a nurse came to visit us.

She told us that every boy and girl in the class would have to get an injection of medicine that day.

All the other boys and girls were afraid, some of them even started to cry. They had never heard of an injection before and they were afraid that it might hurt.

To help the boys and girls understand, Teacher asked if I could come to the top of the class and tell them about my Diabetes and about getting injections.

Even after I had told them my story a lot of the boys and girls were still afraid, so teacher promised that whoever got the first injection from the nurse would win a special prize.

Even with the promise of a prize, no boy or girl was brave
enough to go first. "I'll go first", I said to Teacher and all the
other boy and girls stood back as I walked straight up to the
nurse to get my injection.

My friends couldn't believe how brave I was and cheered and clapped when I went back to my seat.

When everyone had got their injections, teacher called me up to her desk to give me my prize for being the first person in my class to get her injection.

I could hardly believe my eyes! It was a brand new goldfish!

I decided that I would call him Friday, because that was the day that I became known as the bravest girl in school! So what about you? Do you have a special story like mine? Why don't you tell me all about it on your Special Story Page?

Your Special Story Page

SPECIAL STORIES PUBLISHING

Kate Gaynor

Notes for Grown Ups on Diabetes

Diabetes is a condition characterised by high blood sugar levels. It occurs due to a lack of insulin in the body, the hormone responsible for regulating blood sugar.

Type 1 diabetes: This is most common in people under 30 and often appears in early child hood. People with type 1 diabetes are unable to make their own insulin and therefore must be treated with insulin injections.

Type 2 diabetes: This is more common among older people where the body can in fact produce insulin but cannot use it correctly. This type of diabetes can be controlled with correct diet and medication.

As young children commonly suffer from type 1 diabetes it is necessary for them to receive regular injections of insulin. In recent times pen devices have made it much easier for older children to inject their own insulin under parental supervision

How to use this book:

Although parents are of course primarily responsible for the care of their child's diabetes, it is important that the children themselves are aware that they too must take some responsibility. This book encourages children to follow the instructions given to them by their doctors and parents, to eat healthily and also to see their insulin injections as something brave that they do, that other children cannot! Instead of viewing diabetes and their daily injections as something negative, the story encourages them to think of it as something that sets them apart from their peers in a positive way!

For information on Diabetes please contact your local diabetes association.

Other books from Special Stories Publishing

A FAMILY FOR SAMMY: The purpose of this book is to help explain the foster care process to young children.

JOE'S SPECIAL STORY: This story was written to help explain inter-country adoption to young children.

FIRST PLACE: The focus of this book is to help children to understand and accept the effects of cleft palate, cleft lip or any speech impediment in their lives and most importantly, how best to overcome them.

THE WINNER: The intention of this book is to help explain Asthma and its effects to young children.

THE FAMOUS HAT: The aim of this book to help children with leukaemia (or other forms of cancer) to prepare for treatment, namely chemotherapy, and a stay in hospital.

THE LOST PUPPY: This book has been designed to help children with limited mobility to see the positive aspects that using a wheelchair can bring to their lives.

To read more about the special stories collection, visit the Special Stories website at:
www.specialstories.net

39114717R00019

Printed in Poland
by Amazon Fulfillment
Poland Sp. z o.o., Wrocław